Goddess Alchemy 101

Michele Howe Clarke

Copyright © 2023 by Michele Howe Clarke

All rights reserved.

No portion of this book may be reproduced in any form without written permission from the publisher or author, except as permitted by U.S. copyright law.

CONTENTS

1. Goddess Alchemy — 1
2. Understanding Goddess Alchemy — 4
3. The Goddess — 9
4. Unveiling the Immanent Goddess — 12
5. Harnessing Elemental Magic — 16
6. The Unseen and the Seen — 20
7. Goddess as the Tao — 24
8. Embracing Goddess Energy — 27
9. Embodying the Divine Feminine — 32
10. Unleashing Archetypal Energies — 37
11. Goddess Alchemy and Universal Laws — 41
12. Unleashing the Inherent Entelechy — 46
13. Goddess Alchemy and the Law of Attraction — 50
14. Goddess Alchemy and Moon Phases — 55
15. Goddess Alchemy and Twin Flames — 60
16. Goddess Alchemy and Negotiation Success — 65

17. Goddess Alchemy for Prosperity   70

18. Engage Your Thrive Drive   74

19. Thank you, a favor   78

CHAPTER ONE

GODDESS ALCHEMY

Your Spiritual Journey of Transformation

Welcome and get ready to embark on a fascinating journey into the realm of Goddess Alchemy, revealing the Great Goddess with her many aspects and also the little goddess who lives in Y.O.U. (Your Own Uniqueness). The key to Goddess Alchemy is that it puts the power back into your hands and allows that power to work for the highest good of all.

Goddess Alchemy is a spiritual life path that invites you to dive deep into the transformative energies of the divine feminine and the Magic in Y.O.U. Imagine it as a sacred pilgrimage, where you co-create with the goddesses to transmute challenges into wisdom, and stagnation into vibrant growth. So, let's step onto this path and explore how Goddess Alchemy can become your guiding light on a profound spiritual journey of transformation.

Let's begin with a definition of what we are working with here:

Goddess Alchemy - Processes/Technologies/Entrainments to raise vibration and evolve matter. A learning laboratory wherein yourself and the universe evolve.

Many of us are numb, distanced from the intensity of life. An alienated ego can think of wholeness only as the accumulation of more and more matter under its control. Things feel outside so we need more and more.

The Goddess Alchemy is a container and a transformer, taking us beyond dualism. With Goddess Alchemy we are challenged to go inside and move to a greater interiority. As we match our evolution with an involution toward a greater integrity, a oneness in all this separateness.

With Goddess Alchemy 'we are moving beyond ego consciousness not only to an integration of body and mind but a transcendence of body/mind split , to a new level of consciousness based on the dance between soul and spirit.

An Introduction to the Great Goddess from Marion Woodman

Consider the Goddess as the underlying essence that unifies, penetrates, and pervades all things. One goal of Goddess Alchemy is using Her transforming energy into consciousness. To meet Her we allow for her cyclical realm, where she is perpetually destroying and creating. It is time to come to at-one-ment.

To do this we dig through layer upon layer of facades that cover Goddess before we can reach her. Her energy of the collective unconscious allows alchemical transmutation into higher realms of integration.

It is time to connect your inner goddess back to the Great Goddess. Bring back the link between consciousness and the body. Given this potential to grasp our own uniqueness, our own wholeness through the ability to stand alone in togetherness.

Much of our fear stems from the fear of death, our fear of dissolving into nothing. Her very nature of cycles of birth, life, death and regeneration/rebirth is the very darkness we fear. In our fear we feel alienated from the earth, from others and from our deepest feelings.

When we can face the darkness, see the divine immanence of the Goddess in matter, we can establish a balance and a reconnection with our own deepest nature that can root us in a work of meaning and imagination.

Learn to meet the darkness beyond duality and shatter the old ego boundaries to make room the glorious dance of life. Dancing joyfully in her rhythm. In the cosmic dance of life, we believe that every individual possesses the innate power to shape their reality and manifest their dreams.

Chapter Two

Understanding Goddess Alchemy

A Path of Divine Transformation

B efore we begin, let's take a moment to understand what Goddess Alchemy truly means. It's a sacred practice that draws upon the transformative energies of the divine feminine. It's about embracing the power of creation, nurturing, intuition, and empowerment that lies within us all. Think of it as a tapestry woven with threads of ancient wisdom and modern spiritual understanding.

Excerpt from *The Goddess Alchemy Goals Accomplish Planner* **(go gaga!)**

You are engaging the goddess of Y.O.U. (Your Own Uniqueness). By engaging your Thrive Drive you begin to follow your natural lines of growth. Your body's automation is her gift. By understanding your role in creating the environment where you be Peace, Love, Prosper. This is the wheelhouse of your magical powers.

When we each, Magical Sister, engage life as sacred and raise Her gifts in ritual we raise HER energy. As in, we littles goddesses, create the Goddess with a capital G and consciously enliven HER energy better and better is the effect of our cause. Goddess Alchemy, is what I have just described. This is why we practice our magic for the highest good, Magical Sister.

Alchemy is in essence raising vibration. You are raising the energy of your self knowledge. Being into your life as the experiencer and the experienced. There are many resources at your aid. You only need to ask for the help you require. The Goddess is the background of every foreground. She is there always holding everything down, literally. She has you too. Believe.

The Essence of Goddess Alchemy as a companion on your Spiritual Life Path

When you choose Goddess Alchemy as a companion on your spiritual life path, you're committing to a journey of self-discovery, growth, and transcendence of the ordinary to the extraordinary. It's a path that honors the cyclical nature of existence, just like the phases of the moon or the changing seasons. Here, you'll learn to recognize and embrace the ever-flowing energies within and around you.

Embarking on the Path: Opening Yourself to Divine Feminine Energies

The first step on this spiritual journey is to open yourself up to the divine feminine energies. Picture yourself standing at the threshold of a sacred garden, surrounded by an aura of nurturing, creative, and empowering energy. Feel it flow through you, igniting a spark of recognition deep within your soul. It's an invitation to step into your truest, most authentic self.

The Alchemical Process: Transmuting Challenges into Wisdom

As you move along this path, you'll encounter challenges and experiences that may seem daunting. But here's where the magic of Goddess Alchemy truly comes alive. It's about taking those challenges and, with the guidance of the goddesses, transmuting them into wisdom, strength, and personal growth. This process is akin to the ancient alchemists turning base metals into gold—a metaphor for turning the ordinary into the extraordinary.

Embracing the Goddess Archetypes: Discovering Your Inner Wisdom

Central to Goddess Alchemy are the powerful archetypes of the goddesses. Each archetype represents a facet of the divine feminine, offering unique lessons and energies. From the nurturing and compassionate Mother to the fierce and independent Warrior, these archetypes serve as guides, illuminating different aspects of your own inner wisdom.

The Dance of Light and Shadow: Integrating All Aspects of Self

As you progress on this spiritual path, you'll come to understand the dance of light and shadow within you. It's about recognizing and integrating all aspects of yourself—the strengths and the vulnerabilities, the light and the darkness. The goddess energies support you in this integration, encouraging you to love and accept every part of who you are.

The Alchemical Union of Mind, Body, and Spirit

Goddess Alchemy isn't just about spiritual enlightenment; it's about the harmonious union of mind, body, and spirit. It's about recognizing that each facet of your being is interconnected and plays a vital role in your overall well-being. Through practices like meditation, movement, and self-care, you'll learn to nurture this holistic union.

Honoring the Divine in Nature: Connecting with the Earth's Energy

Nature, in all its glory, is a living manifestation of the goddess energies. As you walk this path, you'll find solace and inspiration in the natural world. Take moments to connect with the earth's energy, whether it's through a leisurely stroll in the woods, the feeling of sand beneath your toes, or simply gazing at the night sky. This connection grounds you, reminding you of your place in the grand tapestry of existence.

Rituals and Ceremonies: Nurturing Your Spiritual Practice

Rituals and ceremonies form a significant part of the Goddess Alchemy path. They're like sacred milestones, moments of deep connection and intention-setting. These can be as simple as lighting a candle and meditating, or as elaborate as creating an altar space dedicated to the goddess energies. Through these rituals, you'll deepen your bond with the divine and amplify the transformative energies within you.

Goddess Alchemy Key:

As you walk the path of Goddess Alchemy, remember that it's a journey of self-discovery, growth, and transformation. It's about recognizing the inherent divinity within you and learning to dance in harmony with the energies of the goddesses. This path isn't about reaching a destination; it's about embracing the journey itself.

Through the practice of Goddess Alchemy, you'll come to understand that you are the alchemist of your own existence. You have the power to transmute challenges into opportunities, and to embrace every facet of your being. Trust in the process, and let the goddess energies guide you towards a life filled with purpose, empowerment, and spiritual enlightenment.

So, step boldly onto this path, and let the magic of Goddess Alchemy illuminate your spiritual journey. The goddesses are your companions, and the universe is your guide. Embrace the wisdom that awaits you, and watch as your life transforms into a radiant tapestry of spiritual growth and self-realization. You're on a path of divine alchemy, and the possibilities are boundless. Embrace it, and let your soul shine!

CHAPTER THREE

THE GODDESS

THE ETERNAL CYCLE OF BIRTH, GROWTH, DEATH, AND REBIRTH

In the tapestry of existence, the concept of the Goddess stands as a symbol of cyclical nature, embodying the eternal rhythm of birth, growth, death, and rebirth. This archetype transcends cultures, religions, and epochs, weaving a narrative of life's profound transformational journey. The Goddess represents the inherent wisdom of the universe, teaching us that change is not an end, but a continuous, harmonious cycle. This essay delves into the significance of the Goddess as the embodiment of this unending process of transformation.

The Birth of Life

At the core of the Goddess archetype lies the miraculous act of creation. Like a fertile field, she brings forth life, nurturing it with boundless love and care. This aspect of the Goddess is often portrayed as a mother figure, offering sustenance, protection, and unconditional love to all living beings. In this phase, the Goddess teaches us about the beauty of new beginnings, the potential within every seed, and the nurturing spirit that lies within us all.

The Growth and Blossoming

As life takes root, the Goddess guides us through the phases of growth and expansion. She encourages us to embrace our potential, to reach for the skies, and to unfurl our unique petals. This phase represents the period of self-discovery and personal development, urging us to explore our passions, talents, and ambitions. Through the Goddess, we learn to honor our individual journeys, understanding that each path is a vital part of the greater whole.

The Dance of Death

In the grand scheme of existence, death is not an end, but a transformation. The Goddess embodies this truth, revealing that in every ending, there lies the potential for rebirth. This phase is often depicted through the image of a fierce and transformative goddess, embodying the raw power of destruction. Here, the Goddess teaches us to let go of attachments, to shed old beliefs and patterns, and to embrace the inevitability of change.

The Phoenix's Rebirth

From the ashes of death, the Goddess emerges once more, reborn in a blaze of vitality and newness. This aspect illustrates the eternal cycle of transformation, emphasizing that every ending is a prelude to a fresh beginning. Through the Goddess, we learn resilience, courage, and the unyielding power of the human spirit. She encourages us to rise from the depths, to reinvent ourselves, and to find strength in our own ability to recreate and rejuvenate.

The Eternal Dance

The Goddess as the cycle of birth, growth, death, and rebirth serves as a poignant reminder that life is an ever-evolving, interconnected dance. She invites us to participate actively in this dance, to embrace change, and to recognize that our own transformations are woven into the grand tapestry of existence. Through her, we learn that every phase, no matter how challenging, holds the potential for growth, wisdom, and renewal.

Goddess Alchemy Key

The archetype of the Goddess as the cycle of birth, growth, death, and rebirth is a powerful symbol that transcends cultural and religious boundaries. It is a universal reminder that transformation is not only natural but essential for our personal and collective evolution. By understanding and embodying the wisdom of the Goddess, we can navigate the ebbs and flows of life with grace and purpose, finding solace in the eternal cycle that unites us all. In her embrace, we discover the profound truth that within every ending lies the seed of a new beginning, and within every death, the promise of rebirth.

CHAPTER FOUR

Unveiling the Immanent Goddess

Transforming Your Life, One Step at a Time

The concept of connecting with the immanent goddess energy is a game-changer. Picture this: a life filled with boundless positivity, strength, and wisdom, all flowing from the divine feminine essence within you. Are you ready to make your life better and better? Let's get started.

The Immanent Goddess: Unveiling the Divine Within

First things first, what exactly is this immanent goddess energy we're talking about? It's the belief that the divine, the sacred, the cosmic, whatever you choose to call it, resides within each and every one of us. It's the recognition that we carry within us the very essence of creation and transformation.

You see, this isn't about external deities or far-off celestial beings. It's about acknowledging and tapping into the extraordinary power that resides right here, within our own hearts and souls. It's about understanding that we are not separate from the universe; we are an integral part of it. And that, my friend, is where the magic begins.

Connecting with the Immanent Goddess

Alright, let's get practical. How do we actually connect with this immanent goddess energy and start transforming our lives for the better?

Meditation and Mindfulness Entrainment: Take a moment to sit in silence. Breathe deeply and allow your awareness to settle within. Feel the energy that pulses within you. This is where your journey starts.

Nature Walks: Step outside and let the natural world envelop you. Feel the wind on your skin, listen to the rustle of leaves, and let the earth's energy infuse you. You're a part of this intricate web of life.

Creative Expression: Paint, write, dance, or create in any way that resonates with you. The act of creation is a direct channel to the divine within. Let it flow.

Self-Love and Acceptance: Treat yourself with the kindness and love you would offer a dear friend. Recognize the divinity within you and allow it to shine.

Rituals and Ceremony: Create simple rituals to honor the goddess within. Light a candle, burn some incense, and offer gratitude for the gift of life.

Connection with Others: Recognize the immanent goddess energy in those around you. Treat everyone you meet with respect, knowing that you're encountering another manifestation of the divine.

Mindful Movement: Engage in practices like yoga or tai chi. These activities not only connect your body and mind but also align you with the flow of universal energy.

The Transformative Power of the Immanent Goddess

Now, here comes the real magic. As you continue to connect with the immanent goddess energy, you'll notice shifts occurring in your life.

Inner Peace and Balance: The more you align with this energy, the more you'll find a sense of peace settling within you. It's like finally coming home after a long journey.

Empowerment and Confidence: You'll start to recognize your own strength and power. You'll stand tall, knowing that you are a co-creator of your destiny.

Creative Flow: Ideas will flow effortlessly. You'll find yourself tapped into a wellspring of inspiration that you didn't know existed.

Harmonious Relationships: As you recognize the goddess within, you'll also recognize it in others. This understanding will foster deeper connections and more loving relationships.

Manifestation and Abundance: Your intentions will begin to materialize with greater ease. You'll attract opportunities, people, and experiences that align with your highest good.

Goddess Alchemy Key

So, there you have it. The immanent goddess energy is not a distant concept; it's a living, breathing force within you. It's the source of your power, your creativity, and your ability to shape your own destiny. By connecting with this energy, you're not just improving your life; you're stepping into a realm of infinite potential.

Remember, this isn't about becoming someone else. It's about embracing the extraordinary being that you already are. So, go ahead, tap into that wellspring of divine energy within you, and watch as your life transforms, one beautiful step at a time. You've got this!

CHAPTER FIVE

HARNESSING ELEMENTAL MAGIC

THE 8 DATES OF THE ELEMENTAL WHEEL OF THE YEAR

We're about to delve into something truly enchanting: the 8 dates of the Elemental Wheel of the Year. You might be wondering, what exactly is this wheel, and how can it enhance our yearly outlook and planning? Well, stick around, because we're about to unlock the secrets of this ancient, transformative practice and show you how it can infuse your life with purpose and intention.

Understanding the Elemental Wheel of the Year

Okay, first things first, what is this Wheel of the Year we're talking about? Imagine the year as a circle, divided into eight segments, each representing a significant point in the natural cycle of seasons. These points mark the solstices, equinoxes, and the midpoint between them, celebrating the changing energies of nature. It's a tradition rooted in various ancient cultures, and today, many still observe it as a way to stay in tune with the natural world.

Now, let's break down these eight dates and explore how they can influence your yearly outlook and planning:

Time of Mote: Imbolc (February 1st-2nd): Embracing New Beginnings

Imbolc heralds the arrival of spring's first stirrings. It's a time of cleansing and fresh starts. Take a cue from nature and clear out mental and physical clutter. Set intentions for new projects, nurturing them like tender shoots in the warming soil.

Season of Air: Ostara (March 20th-21st): Welcoming Growth and Fertility

With the arrival of the spring equinox, the world awakens in vibrant colors. This is a time to nurture your dreams and ideas, just as nature nurtures its blossoms. Cultivate creativity, plan ventures, and set the stage for growth and expansion.

Time of Lightning: Beltane (April 30th-May 1st): Celebrating Fertility and Vitality

As summer draws near, Beltane is a celebration of life's passionate energy. It's a time to revel in joy and sensuality, to forge connections, and to celebrate your own vitality. Channel this fervor into your goals and projects.

Season of Fire: Litha (June 20th-21st): Embracing Abundance and Gratitude

At the summer solstice, the world is in full bloom. Take a moment to appreciate the abundance around you. Reflect on your achievements and express gratitude for the progress you've made. Use this energy to amplify your endeavors.

Time of Rainbows: Lammas (August 1st): Harvesting the Fruits of Labor

As summer wanes, Lammas marks the beginning of the harvest season. It's a time to gather the rewards of your hard work and take stock of your achievements. What have you accomplished thus far? Celebrate your successes and plan for the future.

Season of Water: Mabon (September 20th-21st): Finding Balance

At the autumn equinox, day and night are in perfect balance. Take this time to find equilibrium in your own life. Reflect on what needs to be released and what requires nurturing. Create a sense of harmony within yourself.

Time of Mud: Samhain (October 31st-November 1st): Honoring Ancestry and Transformation

As the year comes to an end, Samhain invites us to remember and honor our ancestors. It's a time for reflection, letting go of what no longer serves us, and preparing for transformation. Embrace change and trust in the cycle of life.

Season of Earth: Yule (December 21st-22nd): Embracing Rebirth and Renewal

The winter solstice heralds the return of the light. It's a time to celebrate the promise of new beginnings. Set intentions for the year ahead, envisioning the growth and opportunities that lie ahead.

Incorporating the Elemental Wheel of the Year into Your Yearly Outlook

So, how can you practically use these dates to improve your yearly outlook and planning?

Set Intentions: Align your goals and projects with the energy of each season. Use the vitality of spring to initiate, the abundance of summer to expand, and the reflection of autumn to refine.

Reflect and Release: Use the transitional points to reflect on what you've accomplished and release what no longer serves you. This creates space for new growth.

Celebrate Milestones: Each date offers an opportunity to acknowledge your progress and celebrate your achievements, big or small.

Connect with Nature: Spend time in nature during these key dates. Observe the changes around you and draw inspiration from the natural world.

Goddess Alchemy Key

So, there you have it! The Wheel of the Year is a powerful tool that can enhance your yearly outlook and planning. By aligning your intentions with the natural energies of each season, you can tap into a wellspring of inspiration and purpose. Embrace this ancient practice and let it guide you on a transformative journey through the cycles of life. Happy wheel-turning!

The ancient wisdom that "everything is first worked out in the unseen before it is manifested in the seen" holds a profound truth that transcends time and space. This principle underlines the immense power of thought in shaping our reality. Here, we'll explore how the unseen realm of our thoughts and intentions acts as the cause, ultimately giving rise to the effects we witness in our material world.

CHAPTER SIX

THE UNSEEN AND THE SEEN

CAUSE AND EFFECT

In the grand design of existence, there exists an interplay between the realms of the unseen (cause) and the seen (effect). Our thoughts and intentions are the seeds planted in the unseen realm, which then germinate and blossom into our tangible experiences. Understanding this dynamic empowers us to consciously mold our reality according to our desires.

Transmute with Mind Magic

Take a few moments to sit in a quiet space. Close your eyes and visualize a goal or desire you have. Envision it with as much detail as possible, immersing yourself in the emotions and sensations associated with its realization. This exercise helps anchor your intention in the unseen, setting the stage for it to manifest in the seen.

Evolution and Gradual Development

Just as the universe evolves gradually, so does our individual development. This progression is marked by an ever-increasing capacity and volume. It reminds us that growth is a continuous journey, with each step building upon the last. Embracing this notion allows us to be patient and compassionate with ourselves as we navigate our personal evolution.

Transmute with Mind Magic

Reflect on a skill or quality you'd like to develop within yourself. Break it down into small, manageable steps. Commit to dedicating a portion of your time each day to honing this skill or nurturing this quality. Gradual progress will lead to profound transformation over time.

Mind and Desire: Catalysts of Creation

The mind is a potent force that responds to our desires in direct proportion to the clarity of our purpose and the strength of our faith. This underscores the importance of aligning our intentions with unwavering belief. When our desires are fueled by a deep sense of purpose, the mind becomes a powerful tool for manifestation.

Transmute with Mind Magic

Write down a specific desire you have. Next to it, jot down the underlying purpose that fuels this desire. Take a moment to reflect on the strength of your belief in its realization. If any doubts arise, gently acknowledge them and affirm your unwavering faith in the process.

Thought as a Bridge to Power

Our thoughts are the bridge that allows us to absorb the spirit of power, anchoring it within our inner consciousness. This process transforms the intangible into the tangible, making the power an integral part of our everyday experience. It is a reminder of our innate ability to shape our reality through the focused power of thought.

Transmute with Mind Magic

Choose an affirmation or mantra that resonates with you. Repeat it daily, allowing the words to permeate your consciousness. As you do so, visualize the energy of this affirmation infusing your being, becoming a fundamental part of your thought patterns and belief system.

Empowering Your Magnetic Force

The ancient Hermetics understood the profound significance of attention and intention in the act of creation. In our modern context, we recognize that our minds act as magnets, drawing unto us experiences, circumstances, and energies that resonate with our predominant thoughts and beliefs.

Transmute with Mind Magic

Reflect on the predominant thoughts that occupy your mind on a daily basis. Are they aligned with the reality you desire to create? If not, gently redirect your focus towards thoughts that support your vision.

Like charging a magnet, infuse your mind with the mental energy that amplifies your power of attraction.

As you engage with these exercises and concepts, remember that you possess the innate ability to shape your reality. Embrace the unseen realm of your thoughts and intentions, for they are the architects of your tangible experiences. With focused intention, unwavering faith, and purposeful thought, you have the power to manifest your ideal reality.

Chapter Seven

GODDESS AS THE TAO

Yin and Yang Essence

The concept of the Tao, originating from ancient Chinese philosophy, represents the fundamental principle that is the source of everything in the universe. It encompasses the duality and interconnectedness of all things, emphasizing the flow of energy and the natural order of existence. Traditionally, the Tao has been depicted as a masculine force, symbolized by the Yin and Yang.

In recent years, there has been a growing recognition of the need to incorporate a feminine aspect into the Tao philosophy, acknowledging the vital role of the Goddess in achieving balance and harmony in our lives and the world at large. This shift in perspective invites us to explore how the principles of the Goddess align with the essence of the Tao.

The Goddess as Yin: Nurturer and Source of Life

In Taoist philosophy, Yin represents receptivity, intuition, and the nurturing qualities of the universe. The Goddess embodies these characteristics, offering us a profound understanding of the nurturing aspect of the Tao. Like the Earth itself, the Goddess provides sustenance, support, and unconditional love.

Embracing the Goddess as the Yin in the Tao encourages us to cultivate compassion, empathy, and a deep connection with nature. It calls upon us to recognize the inherent value of nurturing relationships, not only with one another but with the entire ecosystem.

The Goddess as Yang: Empowerment and Creative Energy

The Yang aspect of the Tao is often associated with assertiveness, action, and creative energy. This is where the Goddess reveals her dynamic, empowering side. Through various mythologies and cultural narratives, the Goddess embodies strength, wisdom, and the power to create and transform.

Acknowledging the Goddess as the Yang in the Tao encourages us to harness our inner strength and creativity. It invites us to take initiative, to shape our destinies, and to contribute positively to the world around us.

Embracing the Dance of Yin and Yang

The integration of the Goddess into the Tao brings forth a harmonious dance between Yin and Yang energies. This fusion represents a balanced and holistic approach to life, recognizing the complementary nature of opposites.

By recognizing the Goddess as an essential aspect of the Tao, we learn to appreciate both the gentle nurturing and the fierce strength within ourselves and the world. This acknowledgment leads to a greater sense of self-awareness, acceptance, and a deeper connection to the natural rhythms of existence.

Practical Applications: Honoring the Goddess in Daily Life

Cultivating Compassion: Practice acts of kindness and compassion towards yourself and others. Recognize the interconnectedness of all living beings and the importance of nurturing these relationships.

Creative Expression: Tap into your creative energy and express yourself through art, writing, dance, or any form of creative endeavor. Allow the Goddess's empowering energy to flow through you.

Connecting with Nature: Spend time in nature, observing its cycles and patterns. Recognize the wisdom inherent in the natural world and the nurturing energy it provides.

Balancing Yin and Yang Practices: Incorporate practices that nurture both your receptive and assertive energies. This could include activities like meditation, yoga, or martial arts.

Goddess Alchemy Key

Embracing the Goddess as the Tao invites us to honor and integrate the nurturing, empowering, and transformative energies within and around us. By recognizing the interplay of Yin and Yang in our lives, we can foster balance, harmony, and a deeper connection to the fundamental principles of the universe. Through this integration, we embark on a journey towards a more holistic and fulfilling existence.

Chapter Eight

Embracing Goddess Energy

Navigating Life's Stages with Grace and Wisdom

It is best to move down the stages of life, guided by the radiant energy of the Goddess. Picture this: a life where you move through each phase with purpose, embracing the unique qualities and strengths that come with it. Sounds empowering, doesn't it? Well, buckle up, because we're about to explore how the Goddess embodies different stages of life, and how you can tap into this divine energy to navigate your own journey with grace and wisdom.

The Maiden: Embracing Youthful Enthusiasm

Let's kick things off with the Maiden. This is the stage of youthful exuberance, exploration, and unbridled potential. The Maiden embodies qualities of innocence, curiosity, and a thirst for new experiences. Picture a field of wildflowers, each one representing a new opportunity waiting to be explored.

In your own life, embrace the Maiden by:

Embracing Curiosity: Stay open to learning and trying new things. Approach life with a sense of wonder and a willingness to explore.

Taking Risks: Don't be afraid to step out of your comfort zone. Take risks and trust in your abilities to navigate uncharted territories.

Nurturing Friendships: Cultivate meaningful relationships with others who share your enthusiasm for life. Build a supportive community around you.

Setting Intentions: Plant the seeds of your dreams and goals. Trust that they will grow and flourish with time and attention.

The Mother: Nurturing and Creating

Next up, we have the Mother phase. This is a time of nurturing, creation, and abundance. The Mother embodies qualities of compassion, love, and the ability to bring forth life in various forms. Think of a lush garden, teeming with life and potential.

To embrace the Mother energy, consider:

Nurturing Yourself and Others: Extend the same care and compassion you offer to others to yourself. Remember, self-love is at the heart of nurturing.

Expressing Creativity: Whether it's through art, caregiving, or any form of creation, let your unique expressions flow freely.

Cultivating Abundance: Recognize the abundance around you, both in material resources and the love and support of those who care about you.

Honoring Life Cycles: Understand that creation and growth occur in cycles. Embrace the ebb and flow of life.

The Queen: Embodying Authority and Wisdom

Now, let's talk about the Queen phase. This is a stage of authority, leadership, and wisdom. The Queen exudes confidence, inner strength, and a deep understanding of her own power. Imagine a majestic oak tree, firmly rooted and standing tall.

To embody the Queen energy, consider:

Claiming Your Authority: Recognize and own your strengths and abilities. Trust in your capacity to lead and make decisions.

Cultivating Inner Wisdom: Take time for introspection and self-reflection. Trust your intuition and draw upon the wisdom gained through life experience.

Prioritizing Boundaries: Establish and maintain healthy boundaries in your relationships and commitments. Understand that it's okay to say no when necessary.

Mentoring and Supporting Others: Share your wisdom and experiences with others. Be a source of guidance and support for those who seek your leadership.

The Crone: Embracing Transformation and Wisdom

Finally, we have the Crone phase. This is a stage of wisdom, transformation, and embracing the mysteries of life. The Crone embodies qualities of introspection, acceptance, and a deep connection to the spiritual realm. Picture a wise old tree, its branches reaching towards the heavens.

To embrace the Crone energy, consider:

Embracing Change: Welcome and honor the natural cycles of life, including those of aging and transformation.

Seeking Inner Truth: Delve into spiritual practices that resonate with you. Connect with your inner self and explore the depths of your soul.

Letting Go: Release attachments to what no longer serves your growth. Trust in the process of transformation and the wisdom it brings.

Becoming a Source of Guidance: Share your accumulated wisdom with those who seek it. Be a beacon of light for others on their own journeys.

Goddess Alchemy Key

And there you have it, the four stages of life, each beautifully embodied by the Goddess in her various forms. Remember, these stages aren't confined by age, but rather, they represent the evolving energies within all of us. By recognizing and embracing the qualities of each phase, you can navigate your own journey with purpose, grace, and wisdom.

So, whether you find yourself in the bloom of youth, the nurturing phase of motherhood, the empowering years of queenship, or the reflective stage of the crone, know that you are embodying the divine essence of the Goddess. Trust in the wisdom and strength that reside within you, and let them guide you on your extraordinary journey through life. Embrace the magic that comes with each stage, and may your path be illuminated by the radiant energy of the Goddess. You've got this!

Chapter Nine

EMBODYING THE DIVINE FEMININE

Exploring 8 Goddess Aspects from Around the World

When you need to call upon a strength beyond your own, it is good to have some aspects of the Goddess on your victorious team. They are awaiting your call to come to your aide through Her Energy Rising. Let's keep raising vibration, helping ourselves and all, its such a wondrous win/win.

Let's take a look at the diverse tapestry of goddess aspects that have graced cultures across the globe. We'll be delving into the teachings and energies of two African Orishas, two Egyptian Goddesses, one Hindu Goddess, two European Goddesses, and one Polynesian Goddess. Each of these powerful, divine beings offers us a unique perspective on life, love, wisdom, and transformation. Let's dive in!

African Orishas:

Yemaya - The Nurturer and Protector

Hailing from the Yoruba tradition, Yemaya is a maternal figure, embodying the essence of motherhood, nurturing, and protection. She is often associated with the ocean, its vastness reflecting her boundless love and care for all living beings. Yemaya teaches us the importance of unconditional love, compassion, and the strength that arises from protecting those we hold dear.

Oshun - The Goddess of Love and Creativity

Oshun, also from the Yoruba tradition, is a radiant force of love, beauty, and creativity. She is often associated with rivers, symbolizing the flow of life and the creative energies that spring forth from it. Oshun teaches us the power of self-love, embracing our sensuality, and tapping into our innate creative potential. She reminds us that we are all artists of our own lives.

Egyptian Goddesses:

Isis - The Great Mother and Healer

In ancient Egyptian mythology, Isis is revered as the ultimate mother figure and the goddess of magic and healing. She possesses unparalleled wisdom and the ability to bring restoration and transformation to those in need. Isis teaches us the potency of resilience and the boundless capacity for healing that lies within us all.

Bastet - The Fierce Protector and Warrior

Bastet, another powerful Egyptian deity, is often depicted as a lioness or a woman with the head of a lioness. She represents fierce protection, ferocity in battle, and a deep love for her devotees. Bastet encourages us to embrace our inner warrior, stand up for what we believe in, and fiercely protect our own well-being and that of our loved ones.

Hindu Goddess:

Kali - The Goddess of Transformation and Liberation

Kali, a central figure in Hindu mythology, embodies the raw, transformative energy of destruction and creation. She wields a sword to cut through illusions and a fiery passion that burns away the old, making way for new growth. Kali teaches us that sometimes, in order to grow and evolve, we must be willing to let go of what no longer serves us, even if it is painful.

European Goddesses:

Athena - The Goddess of Wisdom and Strategic Warfare

Athena, from Greek mythology, is the embodiment of wisdom, strategy, and courage in the face of adversity. She is often depicted with an owl, symbolizing her keen insight and foresight. Athena teaches us the value of strategic thinking, the importance of seeking wisdom, and the empowerment that comes from standing confidently in our own abilities.

Freya - The Goddess of Love, Fertility, and Magic

In Norse mythology, Freya reigns as the goddess of love and sensuality. She is associated with fertility, beauty, and the mystical arts. Freya encourages us to celebrate our own sensuality and embrace our desires, recognizing them as a natural and vital part of our being.

Polynesian Goddess:

Pele - The Goddess of Fire, Volcanoes, and Creativity

From the vibrant culture of Hawaii, Pele embodies the fiery energy of creation and transformation. As the goddess of volcanoes, she symbolizes the power to reshape the very land we walk on. Pele inspires us to tap into our own creative potential, recognizing that within us lies the power to shape our own destinies.

Goddess Alchemy Key

And there you have it, a vibrant tapestry of goddess archetypes from diverse cultures around the world. Each of these powerful beings offers us unique insights and teachings, reflecting different aspects of the divine feminine within us all. As you explore these archetypes, take a moment to reflect on the qualities and energies that resonate with you the most. Embrace them, integrate them into your life, and watch as they empower you on your own journey of self-discovery, growth, and transformation. Remember, the wisdom of these goddesses is not confined to the pages of ancient texts; it lives within you, waiting to be awakened and embraced. May their radiant energies guide you on your extraordinary path.

CHAPTER TEN

UNLEASHING ARCHETYPAL ENERGIES

YOUR GUIDE TO PERSONAL DEVELOPMENT

Consider archetypal energy patterns as universal templates that shape our behavior, thoughts, and emotions. Understanding and harnessing these energies can be a powerful tool for personal development. So, grab a cup of tea and let's embark on this enlightening journey!

What Are Archetypal Energy Patterns?

Think of archetypes as fundamental blueprints that exist within the collective unconscious. They're timeless, universal themes that have been present throughout human history. These patterns encompass a wide range of characters, from the Hero embarking on a quest to the Nurturer providing unconditional love. Recognizing and working with these archetypes can shed light on our motivations, desires, and potential for growth.

The Hero: Embracing Courage and Purpose

The Hero archetype is all about embarking on a journey, facing challenges, and emerging transformed. We see this narrative in countless myths and stories. In our own lives, the Hero represents our innate courage to confront obstacles, learn from them, and emerge stronger than before. Embrace your inner Hero by setting goals, facing fears, and daring to venture into the unknown.

The Nurturer: Cultivating Love and Compassion

The Nurturer archetype embodies unconditional love, compassion, and care. This energy is present in parents, mentors, and anyone who provides support and guidance. Cultivating your inner Nurturer involves showing kindness to yourself and others, offering support, and creating a nurturing environment. By tapping into this archetype, you become a source of healing and growth for yourself and those around you.

The Sage: Seeking Wisdom and Insight

The Sage archetype is the eternal seeker of truth and wisdom. This energy pattern encourages us to explore the depths of knowledge, whether through formal education or personal introspection. To embody the Sage, cultivate a curious mind, seek out learning opportunities, and trust in your own inner wisdom. This archetype reminds us that growth is a lifelong journey of discovery.

The Explorer: Embracing Curiosity and Openness

The Explorer archetype is driven by a deep curiosity about the world and a desire for new experiences. This energy invites us to step outside of our comfort zones, whether through travel, trying new hobbies, or exploring different perspectives. To activate your inner Explorer, be open to new opportunities, embrace change, and allow your curiosity to lead you towards personal expansion.

The Alchemist: Transforming Challenges into Growth

The Alchemist archetype embodies the power of transformation and change. This energy pattern teaches us to see challenges not as setbacks, but as opportunities for growth and evolution. To embrace your inner Alchemist, practice resilience, adaptability, and a willingness to learn from every experience. This archetype empowers you to turn life's challenges into catalysts for positive change.

The Creator: Unleashing Innovation and Expression

The Creator archetype is fueled by the desire to bring something new into existence, whether it's through art, innovation, or any form of self-expression. This energy invites us to tap into our creativity and manifest our unique visions. To embody the Creator, engage in activities that allow you to express yourself authentically, whether it's painting, writing, or pursuing a passion project. This archetype reminds us of our innate power to shape our own realities.

The Rebel: Embracing Individuality and Authenticity

The Rebel archetype challenges societal norms and conventions, urging us to embrace our individuality and stand up for what we believe in. This energy pattern empowers us to break free from limiting beliefs and express our true selves boldly. To activate your inner Rebel, question the status quo, celebrate your uniqueness, and advocate for your own authenticity. This archetype reminds us that true growth often requires stepping outside of our comfort zones and embracing our authentic selves.

Goddess Alchemy Key

As you journey through life, consider how these archetypal energies weave into the fabric of your being. Embrace the Hero's courage, the Nurturer's compassion, the Sage's quest for wisdom, the Explorer's curiosity, the Alchemist's transformative power, the Creator's innovation, and the Rebel's authenticity. By recognizing and working with these energies, you'll find a powerful framework for personal development and self-discovery. Remember, you're not limited to one archetype; you have the capacity to embody them all, allowing you to navigate life's challenges and opportunities with grace and purpose. So, go forth and embrace the archetypal energies that resonate most deeply with you. Your journey towards personal growth and self-realization awaits!

CHAPTER ELEVEN

GODDESS ALCHEMY AND UNIVERSAL LAWS

Transforming Your Life into Gold

Goddess Alchemy, a powerful practice that harnesses the energies of the divine feminine to transmute the ordinary into the extraordinary. Goddess Alchemy weaves in the profound principles of Universal Laws, which govern the very fabric of our existence. When combined, these forces become an unstoppable catalyst for positive change and self-realization. So, grab your metaphorical philosopher's stone, and let's dive into the alchemical process of turning your life into pure gold.

Understanding Goddess Alchemy: Embracing Divine Feminine Energies

Before we dive into the alchemical mix, let's first understand what Goddess Alchemy truly is. It's a transformative process that draws upon the sacred energies of the divine feminine. Picture it as a dance with the Goddess, where you co-create with her to transmute the challenges and experiences of life into wisdom, growth, and empowerment.

Universal Law #1: The Law of Divine Oneness

The Law of Divine Oneness states that we are all interconnected, part of a vast cosmic web. In Goddess Alchemy, this law reminds us that we are not separate from the divine or from one another. It encourages us to recognize the divine spark within ourselves and every living being. By embracing this oneness, we tap into a wellspring of compassion, understanding, and unity.

Universal Law #2: The Law of Vibration

The Law of Vibration asserts that everything in the universe, from the smallest atom to the largest star, is in a constant state of motion and energy. In Goddess Alchemy, this law encourages us to attune our energetic frequency to higher vibrations. By embodying qualities such as love, joy, and gratitude, we align ourselves with the divine flow of energy, inviting more positivity and abundance into our lives.

Universal Law #3: The Law of Correspondence

The Law of Correspondence teaches us that the patterns and experiences in our outer world are a reflection of our inner world. In Goddess Alchemy, this law prompts us to explore our inner landscape, recognizing and transforming limiting beliefs, patterns, and thought processes. By aligning our inner reality with our desired outer reality, we unlock the potential for profound change.

Universal Law #4: The Law of Polarity

The Law of Polarity reminds us that duality is a natural part of existence. In Goddess Alchemy, this law encourages us to embrace both the light and shadow aspects of ourselves. It invites us to acknowledge and integrate our perceived flaws and challenges, recognizing them as opportunities for growth and transformation. By finding balance within ourselves, we tap into our full potential.

Universal Law #5: The Law of Rhythm

The Law of Rhythm emphasizes the cyclical nature of life. In Goddess Alchemy, this law encourages us to honor the ebbs and flows of our own journey. It reminds us that periods of growth are often followed by periods of rest and reflection. By understanding and respecting these natural rhythms, we cultivate a sense of patience, trust, and acceptance in our personal evolution.

Universal Law #6: The Law of Cause and Effect

The Law of Cause and Effect, often known as karma, teaches us that every action has a corresponding reaction. In Goddess Alchemy, this law prompts us to take responsibility for our thoughts, emotions, and actions. It encourages us to be mindful of the energy we put out into the world, knowing that it shapes the experiences that come back to us. By acting with intention and integrity, we align ourselves with the flow of positive energy.

Universal Law #7: The Law of Gender

The Law of Gender acknowledges the presence of both masculine and feminine energies within all of us. In Goddess Alchemy, this law highlights the importance of balance and integration. It invites us to honor and nurture our own divine feminine essence, recognizing it as a source of intuition, creativity, and empowerment. By embracing and harmonizing these energies, we tap into a wellspring of personal strength and transformation.

Goddess Alchemy Key:

As we combine the potent energies of Goddess Alchemy with the guiding principles of Universal Laws, we embark on a transformative journey of self-discovery and empowerment. Remember, this process is not about achieving perfection, but about embracing the journey of becoming. It's about recognizing the innate potential within you to turn life's challenges into opportunities for growth and alchemical transformation.

So, step boldly into this alchemical dance with the Goddess, and let the Universal Laws be your guiding stars. Allow them to illuminate your path and infuse your life with purpose, abundance, and radiant empowerment. You are the alchemist of your own existence, and the philosopher's stone lies within your heart. Embrace it, and watch as your life transforms into pure gold. You've got the power, the wisdom, and the divine spark within you. It's time to shine!

Chapter Twelve

Unleashing the Inherent Entelechy

Harnessing Goddess Energy for Personal Transformation

Let's delve deep into the profound wellspring of goddess energy within you. This inherent entelechy, or innate potential for growth and self-realization, is like a dormant force waiting to be awakened. By tapping into this divine essence, you can embark on a journey of personal transformation that will elevate every aspect of your life. So, let's explore how to unleash this inherent entelechy and allow the radiant energy of the Goddess to guide you towards a more vibrant, empowered existence.

Understanding Inherent Entelechy and Goddess Energy

Before we dive in, let's unpack these concepts a bit. Inherent entelechy is the inner drive towards self-actualization and fulfillment, a term coined by the philosopher Aristotle. It's the inherent potential within each of us to evolve and become the best version of ourselves. Now, combine this with the concept of goddess energy, which represents the divine, feminine essence that resides within all of us. This energy is nurturing, creative, powerful, and infinitely wise. When we tap into it, we're drawing upon an ancient, transformative force that can guide us towards our truest, most empowered selves.

1. Embracing Self-Love and Acceptance

The first step in harnessing goddess energy is to cultivate a deep sense of self-love and acceptance. Imagine the Goddess cradling you in her arms, showering you with unconditional love and acceptance for who you are, flaws and all. Embrace your uniqueness, celebrate your strengths, and be compassionate towards your imperfections. Know that you are worthy of love, just as you are.

2. Cultivating Intuition and Inner Wisdom

Goddess energy is intimately connected with intuition and inner wisdom. It's that quiet, knowing voice that guides you towards the right path. To cultivate this, take moments of stillness and introspection. Trust your gut feelings and honor your inner knowing. The more you listen, the stronger this innate wisdom becomes, and the clearer your path in life will be.

3. Tapping into Creativity and Expression

The Goddess is the ultimate creator, birthing galaxies, life, and infinite possibilities. You too possess this creative force within you. Engage in activities that allow you to express yourself freely, whether it's through art, writing, dance, or any form of creative expression that resonates with you. By doing so, you're aligning with the creative energy of the Goddess and inviting new opportunities and experiences into your life.

4. Nurturing and Supporting Others

The nurturing aspect of goddess energy is about extending love and support not only to yourself but also to others. Offer a listening ear, a kind word, or a helping hand. Acts of kindness and compassion create a ripple effect of positive energy that uplifts both you and those around you. Remember, as you give, so shall you receive.

5. Embracing Change and Transformation

Change is a natural part of life, and goddess energy encourages us to embrace it. Just as the Goddess cycles through phases of creation, preservation, and destruction, so too do we go through cycles of growth and transformation. Embrace change as an opportunity for renewal and growth, knowing that it brings you one step closer to your highest potential.

6. Honoring Your Body and its Wisdom

The body is a sacred vessel, a physical manifestation of the Goddess's divine creation. Treat it with respect and care. Listen to its needs and honor its wisdom. Engage in practices like yoga, meditation, or any form of movement that allows you to connect with and appreciate the wisdom that resides within your own physical form.

7. Trusting in Divine Timing and Synchronicities

The Goddess operates outside of the constraints of time as we understand it. Trust in the divine timing of your life. Pay attention to synchronicities and signs that guide you along your path. Sometimes, the universe has a way of aligning circumstances in ways we couldn't have planned, leading us exactly where we need to be.

8. Connecting with Nature

Nature is the living embodiment of the Goddess's energy. Spend time outdoors, connecting with the natural world. Feel the earth beneath your feet, listen to the rustle of leaves, and breathe in the fresh air. Allow the energy of the natural world to rejuvenate and inspire you.

Goddess Alchemy Key

By tapping into the inherent entelechy of goddess energy, you're stepping into your true, empowered self. You're aligning with a force that has been revered and celebrated throughout human history for its transformative potential. Remember, this journey is a personal one, and there's no right or wrong way to embrace your inner goddess. Trust in your intuition and allow the radiant energy within you to guide you towards a life of purpose, fulfillment, and authenticity. You are a manifestation of the divine, and your potential for growth and self-realization is limitless. Embrace it, and watch as your life blossoms into something truly extraordinary. You've got this!

Chapter Thirteen

Goddess Alchemy and the Law of Attraction

Elevating Your Life's Frequency

Let's combine the ancient practice of Goddess Alchemy with the modern wisdom of the Law of Attraction. This dynamic duo has the potential to catapult your life into realms of abundance, purpose, and fulfillment. So, let's explore how the powerful energies of goddess alchemy and the universal law of attraction can work in harmony to elevate your life's frequency and manifest your deepest desires.

Understanding Goddess Alchemy: Tapping into Divine Transformation

Goddess Alchemy is a sacred practice that harnesses the transformative energies of the divine feminine. It's a dance with the goddesses, a co-creation with the universe to transmute challenges into wisdom, and stagnation into growth. Imagine it as a powerful elixir that empowers you to step into your truest, most empowered self.

Unveiling the Law of Attraction: Like Attracts Like

The Law of Attraction, a universal principle, teaches us that like attracts like. It posits that our thoughts, emotions, and beliefs are energetic vibrations that resonate with similar frequencies in the universe. Essentially, what we focus on, we draw into our lives. When we align our thoughts and feelings with our desires, we set in motion a powerful force that brings those desires to fruition.

Step 1: Aligning with Goddess Energy

The first step in harnessing the power of Goddess Alchemy and the Law of Attraction is to align with goddess energy. Picture yourself surrounded by a radiant aura of divine feminine energy, embodying qualities like love, abundance, creativity, and empowerment. Feel this energy permeate every cell of your being.

Step 2: Clarifying Your Desires

Now that you're attuned to goddess energy, take a moment to get crystal clear on your desires. What does your ideal life look like? What experiences, relationships, and accomplishments do you envision? Write them down, and allow yourself to dream without limitations.

Step 3: Cultivating Positive Vibrations

With your desires in mind, focus on cultivating positive vibrations. Imagine your desires as if they've already manifested. Feel the joy, gratitude, and fulfillment that comes with them. This raises your energetic frequency, drawing your desires closer to you.

Step 4: Releasing Limiting Beliefs

Next, it's time to release any limiting beliefs or doubts that may be blocking the flow of abundance. These beliefs act like energetic barriers, preventing your desires from manifesting. Replace them with affirmations that affirm your worthiness and capability to receive your desires.

Step 5: Embracing the Law of Allowing

The Law of Allowing is an essential component of the Law of Attraction. It means letting go of control and allowing the universe to orchestrate the how and when of your desires' manifestation. Trust that the universe has a perfect plan in place.

Step 6: Taking Inspired Action

While the Law of Attraction is powerful, it's not about sitting back and waiting for your desires to drop into your lap. Take inspired action towards your goals. This action is fueled by intuition and aligned with your desires, propelling you towards them.

Step 7: Expressing Gratitude

Gratitude is a potent amplifier of positive vibrations. Regularly express gratitude for the blessings and manifestations in your life, both big and small. This signals to the universe that you're open and receptive to more abundance.

Step 8: Nurturing Patience and Trust

Patience is a virtue in the manifestation process. Trust that the universe is working behind the scenes, aligning circumstances and opportunities to bring your desires into reality. Be open to divine timing, knowing that everything is unfolding perfectly.

Goddess Alchemy Key

As you embark on this alchemical dance with the goddesses and the Law of Attraction, remember that you're not just a passive observer in your life. You're a co-creator, a powerful force of energy and intention. By aligning with the energies of goddess alchemy and leveraging the universal law of attraction, you're tapping into a wellspring of potential and abundance.

So, step boldly into this dance, and let the goddesses and the universe be your partners. With every thought, emotion, and action, you're sculpting your reality. Embrace this power, and watch as your life transforms into a manifestation of your deepest desires. You're a divine co-creator, and the universe is listening. So, dream big, align with your desires, and let the alchemical magic unfold. You've got this!

CHAPTER FOURTEEN

GODDESS ALCHEMY AND MOON PHASES

HARNESSING LUNAR ENERGIES FOR TRANSFORMATION

The two cosmic forces, Goddess Alchemy and Moon Phases, hold immense power for personal transformation and growth. Picture it as a celestial dance, where the goddesses and the moon conspire to guide you on a journey of self-discovery and empowerment. So, let's embark on this magical voyage and uncover how the interplay between Goddess Alchemy and Moon Phases can illuminate your path towards greater fulfillment and purpose.

Understanding Goddess Alchemy: Awaken the Divine Within

Goddess Alchemy is a sacred practice that taps into the transformative energies of the divine feminine. It's a profound journey of co-creation with the goddesses, a process of transmutation where challenges are turned into wisdom, and stagnation into vibrant growth. Imagine it as a mystical elixir, empowering you to step into your truest, most empowered self.

Moon Phases: The Celestial Rhythm of Transformation

Now, let's turn our gaze to the moon, that radiant celestial companion. The moon waxes and wanes, cycling through phases, each imbued with its own unique energy. From the New Moon, symbolizing new beginnings, to the Full Moon, representing culmination and illumination, each phase offers an opportunity for reflection, intention-setting, and manifestation.

New Moon: Seeding Intentions with Goddess Energy

The New Moon marks the beginning of the lunar cycle, a time of fresh starts and new beginnings. This is the perfect moment to align with the energies of goddess alchemy. Picture yourself in a serene garden, ready to plant seeds of intention. What desires do you wish to nurture and grow in your life? Envision them clearly, and imbue them with the nurturing energy of the goddesses.

Waxing Crescent: Cultivating Growth and Potential

As the moon begins to wax, so too do your intentions gain momentum. This phase is all about nurturing your desires and tending to the seeds you've planted. Just like a gardener caring for a budding plant, tend to your intentions with love and care. Trust that they are steadily growing stronger.

First Quarter Moon: Taking Aligned Action

Now, as the moon reaches its first quarter, it's time to take inspired action. This is the phase of building momentum and overcoming any obstacles that may arise. Embrace the goddess's energy of empowerment and strength, knowing that you have the power to shape your reality.

Waxing Gibbous: Refinement and Illumination

The Waxing Gibbous phase is a time of refinement and clarity. Just as the moon's light is nearly at its fullest, so too are your intentions coming into sharper focus. Reflect on any adjustments or refinements you may need to make on your path.

Full Moon: Culmination and Illumination

Ah, the Full Moon—a time of celebration and illumination! Picture yourself under the radiant glow of the goddess's light. Your intentions have come to fruition, and you stand in the fullness of your achievements. Take a moment to bask in this illumination and express gratitude for all that has manifested.

Waning Gibbous: Releasing and Letting Go

As the moon begins to wane, it's time to release what no longer serves your highest good. Just as the goddess embraces change, so too must you let go of what no longer aligns with your path. Trust in the process of release and surrender.

Last Quarter Moon: Reflecting and Refocusing

Now, in the Last Quarter Moon phase, it's time for reflection. What have you learned on this journey? What adjustments or realignments are needed? Take this time to refocus your intentions and prepare for the next cycle.

Waning Crescent: Rest and Renewal

As the moon approaches its darkest phase, it's a time of rest and renewal. Just as the goddess rests after her work is done, so too must you honor the need for stillness and reflection. Trust that this period of rest is a crucial part of the transformative process.

Goddess Alchemy Key

By aligning the energies of Goddess Alchemy with the phases of the moon, you embark on a profound journey of self-discovery and empowerment. Remember, this is a deeply personal practice, and there's no one-size-fits-all approach. Trust in your intuition, and allow the energies of the goddesses and the moon to guide you on your unique path.

As you embrace this cosmic dance, may you find clarity, purpose, and a deeper connection to your own divine essence. The goddesses and the moon are your companions on this journey, and their energies are here to support and empower you. So, step boldly into this dance, and let the magic of Goddess Alchemy and Moon Phases illuminate your path towards greater fulfillment and purpose. You are a cosmic co-creator, and the universe is listening. Embrace the magic that awaits you!

Chapter Fifteen

Goddess Alchemy and Twin Flames

A Divine Dance of Transformation

Let's embark on a mystical journey that intertwines the enchanting realms of Goddess Alchemy with the concept of Twin Flames. This cosmic duo holds the power to transmute the ordinary into the extraordinary, and to ignite a profound transformation in your life. Imagine it as a dance of divine energy and soul connections, guiding you towards self-discovery, empowerment, and the embrace of your truest self. So, let's dive into the alchemical magic of Goddess Alchemy and Twin Flames, and unlock the potential for an extraordinary evolution in your life.

Understanding Goddess Alchemy: Embracing the Divine Feminine Energy

Before we dive into the dance of Twin Flames, let's first explore the captivating practice of Goddess Alchemy. This sacred art taps into the transformative energies of the divine feminine. It's a dance with the goddesses, a co-creation with the universe, where challenges morph into wisdom and stagnation into vibrant growth. Picture it as a mystical elixir that empowers you to step into your truest, most empowered self.

The Dance of Twin Flames: Soul Connections Beyond Time and Space

Now, let's shift our gaze to the ethereal realm of Twin Flames. Twin Flames are believed to be two souls that originated from the same divine spark, split into two physical bodies. They share a profound and often intense connection that transcends time and space. The reunion of Twin Flames is said to bring about a powerful alchemical transformation, pushing both individuals towards spiritual awakening and growth.

Twin Flames and the Divine Purpose

The connection with your Twin Flame often serves a higher purpose in your spiritual journey. It's like encountering a mirror of your soul—a reflection that illuminates both your strengths and areas for growth. This cosmic partnership encourages you to rise to your highest potential, and to support your Twin Flame on their own path towards self-realization.

Goddess Alchemy and Twin Flames: A Symbiotic Dance

Now, here's where the magic truly unfolds. When you combine the energies of Goddess Alchemy with the dance of Twin Flames, you're harnessing a powerful force of transformation. It's a symbiotic relationship, where the divine feminine energies amplify the growth and evolution that naturally occur within a Twin Flame connection.

The Role of Divine Feminine in Twin Flame Alchemy

The divine feminine energies of Goddess Alchemy play a crucial role in the Twin Flame journey. They bring nurturing, intuitive, and transformational qualities to the relationship. Imagine the goddesses as cosmic midwives, guiding you and your Twin Flame through the process of self-discovery and spiritual evolution.

Transmutation through Love and Compassion

Love is the central force in the dance of Twin Flames. It's a love that goes beyond the romantic, transcending human limitations. This love is a catalyst for profound transformation, urging you to release old patterns, heal deep wounds, and step into your true, authentic self. The goddess energies amplify this love, providing a nurturing and supportive environment for growth.

Embracing Shadow Work for Alchemical Growth

In any transformative journey, including the Twin Flame connection, shadow work is a vital component. This involves facing and integrating the parts of yourself that you may have suppressed or denied. With the support of the goddess energies, you're guided through this process with compassion and wisdom, allowing you to transmute past pain into newfound strength.

Balancing Masculine and Feminine Energies

Just as the dance of Twin Flames involves the merging of two souls, it also entails the harmonizing of masculine and feminine energies. The goddess energies of Goddess Alchemy help you tap into your own divine feminine essence, allowing you to find balance and integration within yourself. This balance empowers you to navigate challenges and embrace growth with grace and wisdom.

The Alchemical Transformation: From Separation to Union

The journey of Twin Flames often begins with a sense of separation or longing. This phase, though filled with challenges, serves as a crucible for growth and self-discovery. With the support of the goddess energies, you're guided through the alchemical process, transmuting the raw elements of your experiences into wisdom and self-realization.

Reunion and Integration: The Alchemical Elixir of Love

As you and your Twin Flame progress on your individual paths of growth, you may eventually experience a reunion. This reunion is like the merging of two alchemical elixirs, creating a potent blend of love, wisdom, and spiritual evolution. The goddess energies continue to support this process, nurturing the union and facilitating further growth.

Goddess Alchemy Key

As you embark on this cosmic dance of Goddess Alchemy and Twin Flames, remember that you're not just on a personal journey. You're part of a grand symphony of transformation and love, where each note contributes to the harmonious evolution of your souls.

Embrace the energies of the goddesses, and honor the unique connection with your Twin Flame. Trust in the alchemical process, and allow the dance to guide you towards self-discovery, empowerment, and the embrace of your truest self. You are a part of something extraordinary, and the universe is supporting you every step of the way. Embrace the magic that awaits you!

Chapter Sixteen

Goddess Alchemy and Negotiation Success

Unleashing Your Inner Power

Let's delve into a realm where ancient wisdom meets modern prowess – the art of negotiation infused with the transformative power of Goddess Alchemy. Imagine blending the strength of strategic negotiation with the grace and intuition of the divine feminine. This powerful combination has the potential to elevate your negotiation game to new heights. So, let's embark on this journey of self-discovery and empowerment, and learn how to channel your inner goddess for negotiation success.

The Dance of Goddess Alchemy

Goddess Alchemy is a concept that taps into the divine feminine energy within each of us. It's about embracing qualities like intuition, empathy, creativity, and adaptability, and infusing them into our negotiation approach. Picture Athena's wisdom, Aphrodite's charm, and Kali's fierce determination all rolled into one – that's the essence of Goddess Alchemy.

Intuition as Your Guiding Light

In negotiation, gut feelings can be just as powerful as hard data. The goddess within you possesses an innate sense of knowing, a sixth sense that guides you towards the right path. Trusting your intuition allows you to pick up on subtle cues, unspoken desires, and hidden agendas. It's like having a secret weapon that helps you navigate through complex negotiations with finesse.

Embracing Empathy

The goddesses were known for their deep compassion and understanding. When you step into the shoes of your negotiation counterpart, you establish a connection that transcends mere words. You begin to see the world from their perspective, identifying their needs, fears, and aspirations. This empathy creates a foundation of trust and mutual respect, setting the stage for a more fruitful negotiation.

Unleashing Creativity

Goddess Alchemy encourages you to think outside the box. Imagine yourself as Saraswati, the Hindu goddess of creativity and knowledge. Bring fresh perspectives, propose innovative solutions, and be open to unconventional ideas. This creative flair not only adds value to your negotiation, but it also leaves a lasting impression on your counterpart.

Adapting and Evolving

Change is the only constant, and the goddesses were masters of adaptation. In negotiation, flexibility is key. Like the adaptable water element of Oshun in Yoruba mythology, be willing to flow and adjust your approach as the situation demands. This agility empowers you to seize opportunities and navigate through challenges with grace.

Negotiation Success: A Goddess's Guide

Now that we've tapped into the essence of Goddess Alchemy, let's integrate these qualities into practical negotiation strategies:

Preparation with Purpose

Athena, the Greek goddess of wisdom, was known for her meticulous planning. Before entering a negotiation, arm yourself with knowledge. Research your counterpart, understand their goals, and anticipate potential obstacles. But don't forget to trust your intuition to guide your preparation.

Listening with Heart and Soul

Aphrodite, the Greek goddess of love, possessed an unmatched ability to connect with others. In negotiation, active listening is your superpower. Pay attention not only to words, but also to tone, body language, and underlying emotions. This deep listening fosters a sense of trust and allows you to address your counterpart's true needs.

Engaging in Collaborative Problem-Solving

Demeter, the Greek goddess of harvest, understood the value of cooperation. Seek solutions that benefit both parties, nurturing a sense of mutual gain. Use your creativity to propose win-win scenarios, ensuring that everyone leaves the negotiation table feeling satisfied.

Maintaining Grace under Pressure

Kali, the Hindu goddess of empowerment, embodies fierce determination. There will be moments of challenge and adversity in negotiations. Channel your inner Kali, maintaining composure and assertiveness even in the face of resistance. This unyielding strength will command respect and influence the outcome in your favor.

Goddess Alchemy Key

As you embrace Goddess Alchemy in your negotiation journey, remember that this transformation isn't about becoming someone else. It's about unearthing the powerful, intuitive, and empathetic goddess that already resides within you. By integrating these qualities into your negotiation toolkit, you'll not only achieve greater success, but you'll also leave a positive and lasting impact on those you negotiate with. So, go forth, channel your inner goddess, and let the alchemy of negotiation success begin!

Chapter Seventeen

Goddess Alchemy for Prosperity

Empowering Women Towards Financial Independence

Goddess Alchemy and the journey of women towards financial independence is a topic that's as empowering as it is liberating. We are tapping into ancient feminine wisdom while navigating the modern world of finance. It's like blending the strength of Athena with the entrepreneurial spirit of today's Wonder Women. So, let's embark on this transformative journey and learn how to harness the energy of Goddess Alchemy for financial freedom.

The Essence of Goddess Alchemy

Goddess Alchemy is about embracing the divine feminine qualities within us all. It's like unlocking a treasure chest of intuition, resilience, creativity, and adaptability. Think of it as invoking the ancient goddesses like Lakshmi, Artemis, and Freyja – each embodying unique strengths that we can integrate into our financial journey.

Intuition: Your Inner Guide

In the pursuit of financial independence, your intuition is your secret weapon. It's like having an internal compass that guides you towards the right opportunities, investments, and decisions. Whether it's a gut feeling about a business venture or a hunch about a strategic move, trust your inner voice. It's there to lead you towards success.

Resilience: Weathering the Storms

The goddesses were known for their resilience in the face of adversity. Like Durga, the Hindu goddess of strength, be unyielding in your pursuit of financial goals. There will be challenges, but tap into your inner Durga and face them head-on. Remember, setbacks are just setups for comebacks!

Creativity: Thinking Beyond Boundaries

Creativity isn't just about art; it's about finding innovative solutions to financial challenges. Channel the spirit of Brigid, the Celtic goddess of creativity and inspiration. Whether it's finding new streams of income or crafting unique business models, let your creative juices flow. Break free from conventional thinking and dare to dream big.

Adaptability: Embracing Change

Change is the only constant, and the goddesses understood this well. Like the adaptable water element of Yemaya in Yoruba mythology, be willing to ebb and flow with the tides of the financial world. Adapt to market shifts, embrace new technologies, and pivot when necessary. This flexibility is your ticket to long-term financial success.

Empowering Women Towards Financial Independence: A Goddess's Guide

Now, let's weave Goddess Alchemy into practical strategies for women seeking financial independence:

Education and Knowledge: Athena's Wisdom

Athena, the Greek goddess of wisdom, believed in the power of knowledge. Educate yourself about finance, investments, and entrepreneurship. Attend workshops, read books, and network with like-minded individuals. Let Athena be your guide in acquiring the wisdom you need to make informed financial decisions.

Investing in Yourself: Lakshmi's Abundance

Lakshmi, the Hindu goddess of wealth and abundance, reminds us that we are our most valuable asset. Invest in your skills, talents, and personal development. Take courses, attend seminars, and seek mentorship. The more you invest in yourself, the greater your capacity to create wealth.

Building Multiple Income Streams: Artemis's Independence

Artemis, the Greek goddess of independence, valued self-sufficiency. Diversify your income sources. This might mean starting a side hustle, investing in stocks, or exploring real estate opportunities. By creating multiple streams of income, you build a solid foundation for financial independence.

Embracing Risk: Freyja's Fearlessness

Freyja, the Norse goddess of love and fearless pursuit, teaches us to embrace calculated risks. Don't be afraid to step out of your comfort zone. Whether it's starting a business or making a strategic investment, trust your instincts and take that leap. Remember, fortune favors the bold!

Goddess Alchemy Key

As you embark on your journey towards financial independence, remember that you already possess the qualities of a goddess within you. By embracing Goddess Alchemy, you're not just seeking financial success; you're unleashing your inner power and potential. So, stand tall, trust your intuition, and let the alchemy of financial independence begin! You've got this!

Chapter Eighteen

ENGAGE YOUR THRIVE DRIVE

Access your Navigator

The Thrive Drive of Y.O.U.

The Thrive Drive is an evolutionary stable system over 10,000 years in the making which we, the gifted ones, can leverage for our betterment. It is comprised of Y.O.U and M.E.

Y.O.U. is a supremely intelligent highly responsive automated machine. M.E. is the muscle, the means to enacting your divine design. M.E. is your feet on the street, You see, Your Own Uniqueness (YOU) needs My Excellence (ME) to heed its call and bring it's impetus to life.

Listen, it's all about Y.O.U. Your own uniqueness, the seed of excellence you came programmed with. Like a tiny acorn destined to be a great oak. You have a divine design, an amazing light of your own uniqueness to shine.

When you engage Thrive Drive you access you Navigator. Your Navigator directs you to flow along your natural lines of growth with ease by steadfastly pointing toward your true north. The Navigator of Y.O.U., of Your Own Uniqueness, signals through your internal compass which we interpret as feelings of resistance or flow.

We all seek harmonious flow in our lives. Everybody has their own flow of divine design. AND it's your job to find your flow. It's a mastery thing and you will practice for a lifetime.

Two critical keys of engaging Thrive Drive were revealed:

1)Science has proven that the heart generates the largest electromagnetic field in the body. Your heart is the guide; it is to be deferred to.

Allow yourself to feel it to heal it

2) Research shows shallow rapid breath is connected to higher incidence of anxiety. Breathe is the fastest path to find your flow. It's the express lane to inner peace and resourcefulness.

Exhale, Release, Let go

Breathe in life deeply slow and low

Feel your heart, find your flow

Crisis of Dissipation

We are in a Crisis of Distracted Dissipation. Recent studies show Depression. Type II Diabetes, Drug Dependence in the US are on the rise.

We live in a sea of constant change and data overload. Time seems to go faster and faster and there's always more to do. In the distraction of our harried hurried modern day existence the Thrive Drive is forgotten and can lie dormant for a lifetime.

If we do not decide the cause we intend to effect then we dissipate our precious energy. We drift aimlessly, directionless, at the whim of waves and wind, When difficult situations arise, our flow is too easily interrupted, we get agitated, stressed and we simply react.

Yet all the while the small voice of our navigator is encouraging us, guiding us, giving us permission and praise.

Get in Action

Your divine design shows up as your talents, gifts, abilities, your desires longing for expression, your ideas worth sharing. CHOOSE a desire.

Active faith is demonstrated through the focus of your thoughts, your words, and your actions. Your decision on a point to focus, your imaging of it, and your concentration span toward it are the tools of your causal power. The power to cause the effect you desire to create.

Use of the Thrive Drive is maximized through correct perspective; proper preference and constructive power. Let's tie this together with a set of tools to activate and engage your thrive drive,

Let's AARRCC into it.

Appreciative Awareness:

Pain in life is inevitable but suffering is a choice you make through the stories your perspective tells around the facts of your life.

Use active faith to get behind your automatic reactions. Without judgment, regularly, hourly even; ask yourself if you like the story your perception is telling you?

Realigning Recognition:

If the story does not feel good, your internal compass is indicating resistance. Your flow is interrupted.

It time to get out of your head and into your body.

There is only a millimeter of difference between a stance of confidence and a shadow of doubt.

Relax your brow, pick up your grin
Square your shoulders, lift your chin

Charging Choice:

How large is your self-image container? For that is all that it can ever be filled. Let's create a modern day renaissance and grow our self-images. Lovingly explore your interests across Art, literature, language & music. Be aware that music has a special harmonizing power, when in times of trouble, try humming into it. Bet you have a song in you.

Chapter Nineteen

THANK YOU, A FAVOR

and Next Steps

Thank you for reading this work, it is meant to open your mind to the many aspects of the Goddess and the possibilities inherent in your entelechy, the Magic of Y.O.U.. It is a door to a path to your greatness, your natural lines of growth. I hope you are curious and ready for more. A favor please leave a review so others too can find this path.

Embrace Your Inner Goddess: Dive into the World of Goddess Alchemy at !

Are you ready to embark on a transformative journey towards unlocking your inner goddess and harnessing the power of alchemy? Look no further than www.magicalsister.com – your one-stop destination for all things Goddess Alchemy!

Imagine a space where ancient wisdom collides with modern empowerment, and the result is a vibrant community of like-minded individuals ready to elevate their lives. That's what you'll find at Magical

Sister. We're not just a website; we're a movement, and we want you to be a part of it!

At Magical Sister, we believe that every woman possesses an inner goddess just waiting to be awakened. Whether you're looking to conquer the world of finance, enhance your intuition, or simply connect with a community of empowered women, we've got you covered.

Unleashing the Power of Goddess Alchemy

Goddess Alchemy is the heart and soul of what we do. It's about tapping into the ancient feminine wisdom that resides within all of us. Picture Athena's strategic brilliance, Lakshmi's abundance, and Freyja's fearlessness – that's the energy we're bringing to the table.

Ready to start? Head on over to , and let the magic begin with a special discount for those ready to go gaga. Embrace your inner goddess, step into your power, and let's embark on this incredible journey of transformation and empowerment together. Let's make some magic happen!

www.ingramcontent.com/pod-product-compliance
Lightning Source LLC
Chambersburg PA
CBHW020228090426
42735CB00010B/1621